DANGEROUS MAMMALS

HYENAS

Kim Thompson

NORWOOD HOUSE PRESS

Cataloging-in-Publication Data

Names: Thompson, Kim, 1970-.
Title: Hyenas / Kim Thompson.
Description: Buffalo, NY : Norwood House Press, 2026. | Series: Dangerous mammals | Includes glossary and index.
Identifiers: ISBN 9781978577404 (pbk.) | ISBN 9781978577411 (library bound) | ISBN 9781978577428 (ebook)
Subjects: LCSH: Hyenas--Juvenile literature.
Classification: LCC QL737.C24 T474 2026 | DDC 599.743--dc23

Published in 2026 by
Norwood House Press
2544 Clinton Street
Buffalo, NY 14224

Designer: Rhea Magaro

Photo credits: Cover, p. 1 PlanetWild/Shutterstock.com; p. 6 Nisansala99/Shutterstock.com; p. 7 Federica Cordero/Shutterstock.com; p. 8 EcoPrint/Shutterstock.com; p. 9 John Michael Vosloo/Shutterstock.com; p. 10 Dr. Meet Poddar/Shutterstock.com; p. 12 Renate Engelbrecht/Shutterstock.com; p. 13 Liz Miller/Shutterstock.com; p. 14 Chedko/Shutterstock.com; p. 15 Linda Marie Caldwell/Shutterstock.com; p. 17 Sean Clee/Shutterstock.com; p. 18 neurobit/Shutterstock.com; p. 21 Filipe.Lopes/Shutterstock.com

Printed in the United States of America

TABLE OF CONTENTS

MEET THE HYENA

Hyenas are **mammals**. They look like dogs, but they are not related to dogs.

Their front legs are longer than their back legs. Their teeth and jaws are strong enough to crush bones.

TYPES OF HYENAS

There are four hyena **species**: spotted, brown, aardwolf, and striped.

Spotted hyenas are the largest. They live in southern Africa. They can be six feet (two meters) long and weigh 175 pounds (80 kilograms). Their cries can sound like a person laughing.

Spotted Hyena

Brown hyenas and aardwolves also live in Africa. The brown hyena has thick, straight fur. It has tall, pointed ears and a short tail.

Brown Hyena

The aardwolf looks a little like a fox. Unlike other hyenas, it eats mostly insects.

Striped Hyena

The striped hyena is found in Africa, Asia, and the Middle East.

Scientists know the least about this hyena. It has a bushy **mane** along its back. Black stripes **camouflage** it in tall grass.

FAVORITE FOODS

Hyenas are good at finding food. These **carnivores** have sharp hearing and an excellent sense of smell.

Some hyenas hunt alone. They roam grasslands looking for small prey such as birds, snakes, lizards, and insects.

Some hyenas hunt in packs. Hyena packs can have more than 100 animals!

Packs work together. They take down larger prey such as zebras, gazelles, and baby elephants.

Hyenas are also **scavengers**. They eat **carcasses** of dead animals. This includes meat and bones left behind by lions and other hunters. In this way, hyenas help the environment by keeping it clean.

STAYING SAFE AROUND HYENAS

The Lion King and other stories give hyenas a bad **reputation**. They are actually smart, social animals. They will attack humans only if they are in danger or if food is scarce.

People should not live or camp close to hyenas. They should be extra careful at night, when hyenas are most active.

GLOSSARY

camouflage (KAM-uh-flahzh): to disguise something so that it blends in with its surroundings

carcasses (KAR-kuh-siz): the dead bodies of animals

carnivores (KAHR-nuh-vorz): animals that eat meat

mammals (MAM-uhlz): animals that are warm-blooded, have hair or fur, and feed milk to their babies

mane (mayn): thick hair that grows on an animal's head, neck, and back

reputation (rep-yuh-TAY-shuhn): how people judge and think about someone or something

scavengers (SKAV-uhn-jurz): animals that eat dead animals they find

species (SPEE-sheez): a group of animals that are alike and that can have babies together

THINKING QUESTIONS

1. Where do hyenas live?
2. What are the four species of hyenas?
3. Describe the spotted hyena.
4. How do hyena packs work together?
5. What does it mean to be a scavenger?

INDEX

ABOUT THE AUTHOR

Kim Thompson has been an animal lover ever since she was little. She loves to watch animals and photograph them, especially in the wild. She thinks that learning about animals can inspire people to take actions that help animals survive on the planet we share.